McFarlin Library
WITHDRAWN

William Beltz

By Ellen Wolfe

DILLON PRESS, INC.
MINNEAPOLIS, MINNESOTA

©1975 by Dillon Press, Inc. All rights reserved

Dillon Press, Inc., 500 South Third Street
Minneapolis, Minnesota 55415

Printed in the United States of America

Library of Congress Cataloging in Publication Data

Wolfe, Ellen.
  William Beltz.

  (The Story of an American Indian)
  SUMMARY: A biography of the American Eskimo who became president of the first Alaskan state senate.
  1. Beltz, William, 1912-1960—Juvenile literature.
2. Alaska—Politics and government—1867-1959—Juvenile literature. 3. Eskimos—Alaska—Juvenile literature.
[1. Beltz, William, 1912-1960.   2. Alaska—Politics and government—1867-1959.   3. Eskimos—Alaska—Biography]
F909.B45W64   328.798'092'4 B   92   75-17744
ISBN 0-87518-044-2

WILLIAM BELTZ

As William Beltz grew up in the mining towns of northern Alaska, he observed the unequal treatment of the native Indians and Eskimos in the territory of Alaska. Part Eskimo himself, Will worked to improve conditions and to obtain equal rights for his people. As a member (and later president) of the Alaska Carpenters Union and as a member of the territorial senate, Will worked to change the unequal laws and also assisted in the push for Alaska statehood.

In 1958, when statehood was declared, William Beltz was unanimously elected president of the first senate of the State of Alaska, a great tribute from his fellow senators. He died in 1960 at the peak of his career, but the effects of his work as a representative, a union leader, and a spokesman for the Alaska Eskimos are still felt in Alaska.

Contents

I   THE PEOPLE   page 1

II   NO HELP FOR A BROTHER   page 14

III   SHADOWS ON THE SNOW   page 18

IV   GROWING UP   page 23

V   THE BEAR   page 29

VI   ALASKA IN WARTIME   page 36

VII   WILL RUNS FOR OFFICE   page 43

VIII   TAXES AND FAIR WAGES   page 46

IX   PRESIDENT OF THE FIRST STATE SENATE   page 52

CHAPTER 1

The People

During the last ice age, land joined the Asian and North American continents in the area now covered by the waters of the Bering Strait. Scientists call this ancient land bridge *Beringia*. It was a thousand miles wide and inhabited by great herds of grazing animals. The ancestors of the American Indians may have wandered across Beringia in search of game 28,000 years ago. As time passed, ice blocked off the route between the continents. Then the ice melted, and Beringia was covered by the rising waters. It is thought that about eight thousand years ago the Eskimos crossed the Bering Strait at a point where the sea is only fifty-seven miles wide, breaking their journey at the Diomede Islands. They gradually worked their way eastward, and today Eskimos live in the far northern parts of the land masses circling the North Pole.

Along the top of the world from east to west, there are Eskimos in Greenland, Canada, Alaska, the islands in the Bering Sea, and the northeastern tip of Siberia on the continent of Asia. They resemble the people of northern Asia, with their light brown skin, wide faces, and high cheekbones. Eskimos are not a group of American Indians. They are classified racially as belonging with the northern Asians. They call themselves *Innuit,* "the People."

The life of the Alaskan Eskimos was, and still is, shaped by the climate in which they live. In the north, wintry conditions prevail for as long as nine months of the year. High winds, snow, and temperatures which average thirty to forty degrees below zero frequently make outdoor activity an ordeal for survival. Within the boundary of the Arctic Circle, the sun does not rise from November to mid-February.

The northern woodland gradually gives way to *tundra,* the vast plains of the far North. Trees become smaller, and they are bent by winds and snow. At the very edge of the forest, they are only so many little sticks. A willow or birch tree may grow only as high as a man's knees. Here and there they dot the tundra, a land which receives so little moisture that it would be a desert if not for the *permafrost,* a layer of ground which is always frozen. Only the top foot or two of earth thaws during the brief Arctic summer. The cementlike permafrost keeps the water from melting snow on the surface to nourish the mosses, shrubs, wildflowers, and lichens that burst into life.

The harsh climate both necessitated the lifestyle of the Eskimos and preserved it by isolating them from other groups. No other people built homes like theirs, dressed like them, or ate the same foods they did. The short growing season did not encourage them to raise crops. They relied on hunting to provide them with food other than the small amounts of wild plants they could gather during the summer. Lacking wool and cotton for making cloth, they made all their clothes from the skins and furs of animals. Since wood was scarce, they heated their homes and cooked their food over seal oil lamps.

3 THE PEOPLE

Let's go back in time and follow the Eskimos through one year to see how they planned for survival and overcame the shortage of materials that we might consider necessary for life.

As spring came to Alaska, the Eskimos were in their winter home. They lived in a small house called an *igloo*. It had one room and additional areas for storage. There was an entry passage lower than the house itself. Thus, warm air, which rises, stayed in the living area and did not escape through the entrance. The igloo was made of *sod,* the top layer of ground which is firmed into a thick mat by the roots of plants. This is one building material

Workmen lay sod on the platform that will later serve as the sleeping and sitting bench inside the igloo.

that was plentiful on the tundra. The sod may have been supported by a framework of wood, stone, or even whalebone. Inside, there was a large dirt platform which the family used as both a seat and a bed. Smaller platforms were used as tables.

The April sun held promise, but it was a hard time for the village since hunting was poor. Even the fish were thin from the rigors of the winter! The seals wriggled out of the water to sunbathe on the ice, and the Eskimo hunters had to use all their skill to hunt them. A seal naps lightly, and it was difficult to get within harpoon range. It might take hours of creeping over water-covered ice to get close enough. If spotted by his prey, a hunter could only lie motionless, hoping to pass for a seal. All too often, the seal would slip into the water and dive out of sight.

The spring thaw came late to the tundra. Patches of bare ground peeked through the snow in May. Although the sun shone throughout the nighttime hours, frost might linger until late June.

After the snow had melted, the plains came to life. Fields of flowers bloomed in the never-ending sunshine. Eager for fresh food, the Eskimo women gathered wild celery, ferns, sourdock, and *naskobaguak,* which are spinachlike greens. These plants were harvested in the spring while they were still young and tender.

The people in the village prepared for the food-gathering activities in the summer to come. They traveled during the summer, hunting and gathering food for the winter ahead. While wandering, they pitched tents of sealskin or caribou hide. If they left before the thaw, they might start out by dogsled and leave their sleds on the trail when the thaw

An Eskimo fishing camp near Nome, Alaska.

came. Then they would have to load their possessions on their backs. Even the children and dogs would carry packs. Throughout the rest of the warm season, they would leave excess food and materials in wood caches. They might pick them up on their way to the village in the fall or get them by dogsled after the snows came.

If the Eskimos took a coastal route, they might move their belongings in a *umiak,* which was an open boat holding several people. The boat had a sealskin-covered wood frame and moved through the water with oars or paddles. It was used for moving camp, long trips, whaling, and hunting walruses. It traveled in a fleet with *kayaks,* smaller canoe-like boats holding one man. The kayaks broke up the waves around the umiak, making it safe to move the larger craft through rough water.

Fish and game were plentiful in summer. Runs of

herring came to the rocky seashore to spawn. Salmon also swam from the sea up rivers and streams to their birthplace where they spawned. The men caught the fish in a basket trap of split driftwood. They dammed the streams to catch salmon. Forked spears and nets were also used for fishing. The women dried and salted the fish and dried seaweed to use for food in the coming winter.

Caribou, large deer which are related to the reindeer, came back to the plains from the woodlands where they had wintered. The Eskimos hunted them with spears or bows and arrows. Sometimes the women and children herded the caribou toward the hidden hunters. The meat that was not eaten was dried and cached for winter. The children hunted wild geese, ducks, ptarmigans (a type of grouse), and other kinds of birds with blunt-tipped arrows. Young girls wandered in search of eggs.

The men went to sea in kayaks to hunt walrus, seals, and whales. The kayak was made so that it could turn over in the water without losing its passenger. Capsizing could prevent a man from being injured by a heavy wave in rough water. Both man and boat were covered with waterproof sealskin. A wooden ring held the man in the boat, and he tied his jacket to the edge of the ring. Large sea animals were hunted with harpoons. The harpoon had a tip made from stone or bone. This tip was removable so that if the animal got away, the hunter still had the shaft. For hunting on the water, a sealskin line was fastened to the tip.

The sun began to dip beneath the horizon once again in July. As summer turned into fall, Eskimo women looked ahead to winter and repaired and made clothes with the

A hunter heads out to sea in a kayak.

materials provided by hunting. The skins from wild geese, sewn with the feather side in, made warm booties and undershirts. The women might have made fox-fur shorts for themselves, which were worn with high sealskin boots, called *mukluks,* covering the length of the leg. The men's boots were knee high and may have been worn with bearskin trousers. Eskimos traditionally layered their clothing for the same reason people dressing for cold weather do so today: air warmed by the body is trapped between the inner and outer layers of clothing. The Eskimos made their inner garments with the fur side against their skin and outer garments with the fur side out.

Caribou skin was a favorite material for clothing because it is both warm and lightweight. About eight caribou hides were needed to make a man's double-layered winter suit, and the suit weighed as little as ten pounds. The skins of seals and polar bears were also used. Fox fur was popular for trim, and the women could make beautiful patterned borders by alternating different-colored pelts.

When the tundra wore its autumn colors, the women gathered the brown crunchy roots of sedge, cotton grass, and horsetail. These grasses are placed between the boot and stocking to provide insulation from the cold in winter. The grass padding was changed daily, so the women had to make sure they had a good supply.

As winter approached, the Eskimos moved to permanent quarters and took up village life again. Although they had preserved some food from their summer wanderings, the men still had to hunt throughout the winter. As the sea froze, they used dog sleds to travel over the land-fast ice to the pack ice and open water where the seals were found.

A hunter might have stayed for hours by a breathing hole in the ice, waiting for a seal to surface. Fish were caught throughout the winter through holes chopped in the ice. Traps were set for foxes and hares.

While on the trail, hunters could build a snow house in an hour or two to provide them with shelter. It was made of blocks of snow laid in circular rows. Each layer was smaller than the one before it, so that the finished building was dome shaped. A hole for ventilation was left in the top. The cracks were filled with snow, and then a thin layer of snow was spread over all. The body heat of the hunters and an oil lamp made the snow house snug for a couple of days. After the inside of the igloo became glazed with ice, the hunters built a new shelter.

When the hunters returned, the villagers took a share of the fresh meat, although the man who killed a particular animal would have first choice.

Fresh meat was precious to the Eskimos since their survival depended on it. It was not unknown for an entire village to starve in a winter when hunting was poor. In times of famine, families allowed their infants to die quickly of exposure rather than endure the slow death of starvation.

Even when food was plentiful, nothing was wasted. The traditional Eskimo diet was nutritious just because they did not discard any edible parts of the animals they killed. They ate the marrow, sinews, blubber, heart, liver, and skin of the walrus and seal. The raw skin of the white whale and the narwhal is as rich in vitamin C as oranges are. The Eskimos made a soup of hot water and seal blood. The vegetation that makes up the undigested contents of a caribou stomach was considered a delicacy. Blubber was a favorite treat. "Eskimo ice cream" was made of whipped blubber and salmon eggs or berries.

Since it took a long time to cook meat, Eskimos frequently ate it raw. They cooked and heated their homes with lamps carved from soapstone. Seal oil was used as fuel, and moss served as a wick. The lamps must have kept the igloo comfortably warm since the Eskimos usually did not wear clothes indoors to allow their garments to dry on large drying racks.

The Eskimos spent the long, dark winter enjoying family and community life. They visited back and forth, told stories, played games with their children, and feasted when hunting was good. They held parties at which they danced and sang. Each person "owned" the songs he sang, and no one else could use them. He inherited some of them—these songs may have been so old that no one in the audience could understand their full meaning any more—and he made others up. Singing had a purpose other than pure enjoyment. The Eskimo language was a spoken language. Since the people did not write, songs that told a story served as their newspapers and history books. Other songs made fun of people. The Eskimo singer honed the insult to a fine edge in these songs. Sometimes they had a lampoon song contest to settle a disagreement. The person who became angry at the insults first lost his case.

One game they played that you may recognize was cat's cradle. They wound thong or sinew string into intricate shapes held between their hands. This game was played for many, many years. One traditional figure "drawn" with string was the mammoth, an animal that has been extinct for ten thousand years.

11 THE PEOPLE

Another wintertime activity was the carving of tools and weapons. The Eskimos carved them from teeth, nails, bones, ivory walrus tusk, and soft soapstone. They made needles, spoons, food dishes, and toys from these materials. A soapstone pot might take a month to make. It was chipped from the stone with a cutting tool and smoothed by rubbing the surface with a hard stone. Some utensils were carved in the shapes of animals. Other animal shapes were carved in time of famine in hopes that the carving would make the

Using a hand-fashioned drill, an Alaska Eskimo carves graceful figures from chunks of ivory.

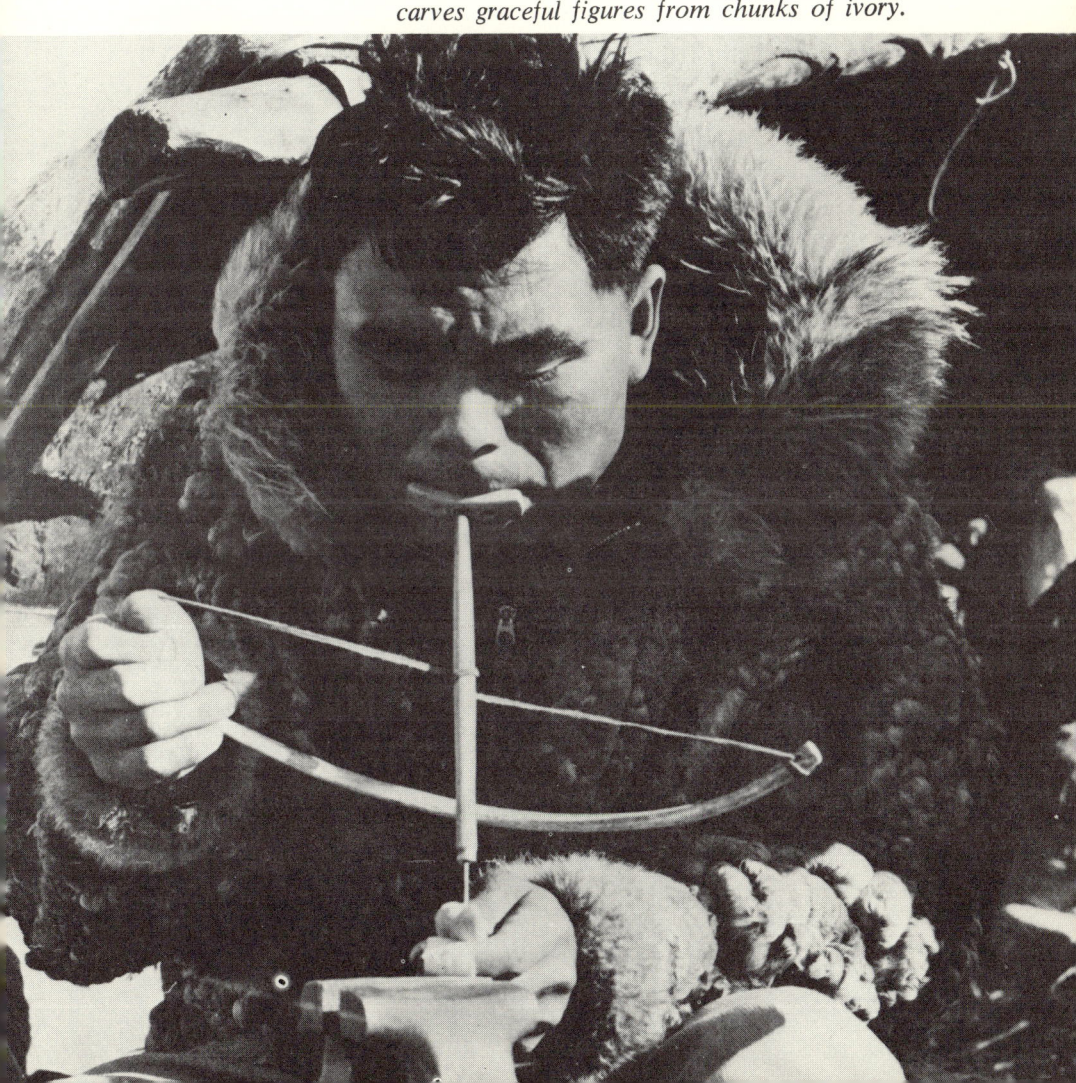

animal appear. Still others were worn as good luck charms. Eskimos also wove baskets from dried sweet grasses. First, the grass was chewed to soften it, and then the blades were woven tightly to make the container. Decorations were added with designs painted in different-colored berry juices.

The Eskimo family was large: there might be as many as twenty members. A household would consist of an older couple, their sons and their sons' wives, and their grandchildren. Eskimos had a short childhood since they took on adult responsibilities of hunting and marriage when they were as young as fourteen.

Perhaps because life was so difficult, Eskimo children were especially treasured by their parents. A newborn baby was given the name of the last family member to die, and it was believed that his or her soul entered the body of the infant to act as its special guardian during the childhood years.

Parents rarely scolded, and never spanked, their children. They felt that a child would learn from experience and observation what was good and what was bad. Eskimo children were encouraged to be independent. They slept when they were tired, and ate when they were hungry. Warmly dressed in two fur suits, they might play outside in the depths of winter from morning to night.

An Eskimo village had no government. Since the land and its resources belonged to all, there were no laws. The villagers shared their food. On the trail, it was understood that if a person was starving, he might break into a food cache. Theft was almost unknown. When disputes occurred, they were settled by fighting or by ridicule, as in a lampoon song contest. If one person killed another, it was up to the victim's family to seek revenge. If an individual was especially prone to violence, the village might decide to put him to death in order to keep the peace. Except for occasional skirmishes with the Indians, the Eskimos never fought in groups. In 1915, when anthropologist Diamond Jenness was collecting Eskimo songs, he asked one group for a war song. They asked him what he meant, and when he explained, they were horrified to discover that men would massacre their own kind.

The religious beliefs of the Eskimos sprang from their feelings about their hostile surroundings. They believed that nature was ruled by spirits, some of them evil. Likewise, each person and animal that died had a spirit. Animals killed for food had to be treated with great respect. Even the game of cat's cradle had its spirit. If, for example, a hunter offended the spirit, it might punish him by causing the line from his harpoon to entangle him as he threw the weapon and sweep him into the water after his prey.

The spirits could bring good hunting or famine to the Eskimos; they could make people sick or help them to get well. A wise man or woman, called an *angatkuq* by the Eskimos, and a *shaman* by white people, had the power to talk with the spirits and ask for good fortune. The Eskimos needed good fortune, for their very lives depended on the chance migrations of animals and suitable weather for hunting.

Our story begins with a little boy growing up in mining towns in northern Alaska. Like his Eskimo ancestors, he knew the tundra, the sea, and the bitter winter cold. He knew the dangers of the ice and heard the howling of the wolves.

CHAPTER II

No Help for a Brother

The cracking sounded like a rifle shot and was loud and clear in the cold air. But sometimes a snap or a pop was the only sign that another hunk of ice had broken away in the ice pack and was free to drift down the Kiwalik River.

It was the middle of May, and the spring thaw was beginning in Candle, Alaska. The river, frozen solid and thick all winter, was now coming apart. This was a big event for the village children. They stood on the banks of the river, and watched the large hunks of ice—called *floes* —drift by, bumping into other floes that were stuck on a bank or a sand bar. Among the children was little Willy Beltz, who was eight years old. He was part Eskimo, and he had always lived in this frozen country. He looked forward to the spring thaw as much as any youngster standing on the bank that day.

One of Willy's younger brothers, Albert, who was seven years old, jumped onto a floe that was stuck on the bank, and then leaped onto another that was just slipping free. His brother John followed, and he nearly missed the second floe with his jump. When he picked himself up, Albert was already standing on the edge of that floe ready to spring

15 NO HELP FOR A BROTHER

to the next hunk of ice that would come by.

The children on the shore, both Eskimo and white, watched closely. They, too, wanted to ride the floes but were scared of slipping off or getting lost down the river. Worst of all, one could fall down the waterfall at the dam downstream.

John and Albert jumped left, and then they jumped right. Each time, they got closer to the middle of the river where the floes went fastest. Willy was proud of his brothers, but he was also a little afraid for them as they continued their leaping. The other kids watched closely and sometimes they cheered when the two brothers made a long jump.

Suddenly, as Albert jumped for the next floe, the ice hunk he was on tipped up swiftly, dumping both him and John into the chilling water. The two struggled and called for help as the cold water quickly soaked their parkas and made their bodies numb. They wanted to swim, but they couldn't move their arms or legs. As the two brothers shouted in terror, the people remained standing on the bank, unable to move. No one—not even their mother who had run up in time to see the boys fall in the river—knew how to swim. As everyone on shore began to shout for help, the townspeople dropped whatever they were doing and ran to the river bank. The two boys were drifting down the river, holding to the edge of an ice floe. Sometimes they disappeared from sight for a few seconds.

Willy ran along the river bank. John and Albert were his brothers; he had to try to help them, but he didn't know how! So he kept running along the bank, ready to do something if he got a chance.

One of the men from town ran down to the dam. He

took a long pole and gave it to John who caught hold. The man pulled him ashore and he was safe.

Albert had disappeared. Willy couldn't even remember the last time he had seen his brother in the water. The men from the village searched for him with long poles. Finally, they found Albert on the bottom of the river near the dam. He was dead.

That night, Willy and his brothers and sisters were sent to the movies so they could forget about Albert for a little while. As Willy watched the movie, he tried not to think about the accident. But Albert was dead and John had almost died because no one knew how to help. Shouting, screaming, and crying hadn't saved Albert.

As he grew up, Will did not forget the death of his brother, and his own feeling of helplessness. Many times, it seemed to him that when people needed help, it was not available. This was true in emergencies, such as Albert's drowning, but it was also true in other situations. When people needed good houses to keep out the deadly Arctic cold, there was no money for the houses. When people needed medical help, there were no doctors or hospitals. As he grew older, Will noticed that many things were needed in northern Alaska where he lived. He began to realize that he would have to learn about a great many things.

Today, only a few years after his death, the story of William Beltz stands as an example of courage and devotion to other people. During his lifetime, as a tribute to his work, he was elected the first senate president of the first state legislature of Alaska.

Will was half Eskimo and half white. He grew up knowing the ways of whites and the ways of Eskimos. Will also learned at an early age that there were two sets of laws: one for whites and one for Eskimos and Indians.

Although they had lived on and used the land of Alaska for centuries before whites came, Eskimos could not get title to land and could not file mining claims as whites could. Eskimos could not sit in the same section of the theater as whites. They could not eat in some of the same restaurants. They could not get jobs that whites could, and if they did get jobs, they were almost always paid less.

Will knew these things were not right. His people were citizens of the country and paid taxes just as white men did. Certainly, they should have the same rights and privileges.

All his life, Will worked to improve conditions and to get equal rights for his people. He fought for representation for them, and in the end served Eskimos, Indians, and whites in the government, and was a respected leader for all people in the state.

CHAPTER III

Shadows on the Snow

William Beltz was born in Bear Creek, Alaska, in 1912. Bear Creek was a small mining camp in the north of Alaska. Willy's father was a miner, and Willy's father, mother, four brothers, and two sisters traveled between mining camps during the year.

The mining towns that Willy grew up in were just a few miles below the Arctic Circle and only about seventeen hundred miles from the North Pole. On one side was the huge, cold Bering Sea, and on the other side were thousands of square miles of frozen tundra.

Growing up in the far North, or the Arctic as it is also called, was very different from growing up elsewhere in the United States. For many years, there was no electricity nor any telephones. So, of course, there were no radios or electric heaters, either. Water did not come out of a faucet. It had to be melted from huge chunks of ice that were chopped out of the river.

Willy knew from stories his mother and father told him that few white men had come to this frozen land before the time when gold was discovered. Then, at the end of the 1800s, the first hordes of miners came to the North during the spectacular Klondike Gold Rush in Canada's

A mining town in the days of the gold rush.

Yukon Territory. Later, gold was discovered in Alaska, too, including the area where Willy grew up. Miners flooded into Alaska, traveling more than one thousand miles from the nearest large seaport by dogsled or by riverboat. Others came during the summer by ship over the Arctic Ocean. These men began setting up mining towns wherever they could find gold.

Willy was fascinated by the miners, for they came from

all over the world. It was hard for him to imagine places so different from northern Alaska. He walked around the areas where the miners gathered and looked at the brawny, weathered men with their big boots and heavy clothing. They all talked about the same things—gold, claims, and fantastic riches—but they talked in different languages. Willy soon decided he would like to see some of these strange places the miners came from.

Willy's father, Jack Beltz, had come more than five thousand miles from Pennsylvania to mine gold out of the frozen ground. He liked the land and the people, and he settled down to work and raise a family. His wife, Susie, was an Eskimo. Her ancestors had lived in this land for centuries. The Eskimos knew the land well: they knew how to survive the cold, and how to hunt and fish to stay alive. Susie told tales of brave Eskimo hunters who had lived long before the white men came.

From his mother, Willy learned the ways of the Arctic. The cold could be deadly, and many men who did not know how to live here died from the cold or lost fingers or toes from frostbite. A man could disappear in this vast wilderness and never be heard from again. Susie taught Willy and the other children to know and respect the land and to protect themselves from its dangers.

Willy's family stayed in Candle during the winter because this was one of the few mining towns that had a school. The winters in Candle were always severe, but there was one winter that was unusually cold. Both men and animals went hungry, and springtime seemed far away. One morning during this hard time it was very cold—sixty degrees below zero. Willy walked to school as always, down the one dark main street. Willy knew it was very cold because his nose froze every time he took a breath. He wore a heavy fur parka, fur mittens, and big fur *mukluks,* which were knee-high boots his mother had made for him out of caribou hide. Usually, these clothes kept him pretty warm, but this morning, as he started to walk down the street, he could feel his hands and feet grow numb.

School was on the far side of town. The huddle of low houses was nearly covered with snow, and everyone was still inside, keeping warm. He could hear nothing but the slight swish of snow as he walked through it. It was very quiet, and very dark, and very cold.

Suddenly, Willy heard the howls of wolves. He shivered. Usually the wolves did not come close to town, but this winter had been so hard that they hadn't been able to find enough to eat. Close to town, they might find scraps of food. The wolves were dangerous, particularly when they were so hungry. As he listened to the sounds, Willy felt like running, but he knew that he would freeze his lungs by breathing too hard and drawing in the cold air so fast.

Willy could just begin to see the outlines of the school in the distance. The howling seemed to be getting closer. He thought he heard rustlings of snow beyond the row of buildings. He felt he might be imagining the sounds, but he wasn't at all sure.

Then, in a clearing about two hundred feet away, Willy saw two shadows. He knew they were real, and he knew he had better get indoors. Should he try to get to school, or return to town and find a safe place to stay? He looked back. It was almost as far back as it was to the school-house. Now, even more than before, Willy wanted to run, but that would be the worst thing to do. It was too cold, and running would just bring the wolves in faster.

Suddenly he felt a tugging at his feet, and he jumped with fright. When he turned around, he found one of his neighbor's sled dogs cringing at his feet with his tail between his legs. Sled dogs were usually tied up, but this one must have gotten free. Willy could see that the dog was very much afraid. Even though a sled dog is a large animal, it is no match for a wolf.

The howling continued. Willy could see more shadows in the distance, and he knew he and the dog had better find shelter fast. Steadily, he walked on. Except for the howling, it was very quiet, and it seemed that no one was around to help. Willy's feet were colder now, and the dog had a mustache of ice around its mouth.

Willy could just make out the shadows as they moved closer. Occasionally, a pair of eyes would sparkle. School was a little nearer, but not near enough.

Suddenly, a shot rang out in the quiet air. A man hurried in Willy's direction. "Did you see the wolves?" he shouted. Willy said yes, he thought he had, and he and the man walked toward where the shadows had been. Wolves certainly had been there—on the ground lay a big wolf with a thick fur coat. The animal was skinny, as though it hadn't eaten for a long time.

The man told Willy he had been very brave not to panic and run, but Willy had not felt brave. His school looked warm and inviting, so Willy hurried on to his classes as the man picked up the wolf.

CHAPTER IV

Growing Up

"Willy! Come here! Mother wants us to get ice from the river before dinner."

Willy and his sister Laura were responsible for getting the ice which the family would melt and use for drinking water. Sometimes, they hauled wood and coal for the big stove that kept the cabin warm. As his sister called, Willy came hurrying up. Chopping ice was work, but it was fun too. Willy could usually get Laura to give him a ride on the sled.

Laura and Willy pulled the sled out from the back of the cabin. They loaded it with large kerosene cans to fill with ice, and long ice picks to use in chopping the ice out of the river.

The two chipped away, and soon they had the cans full. When they finished, Willy hopped in the sled, and he and Laura hurried back to the cabin their father had built for his family. Their home was made of timber. It had the stove in the center for cooking and warmth. The cabin was large enough for the entire family, and the stove would keep everyone warm even on the coldest days.

Susie was cooking when Willy and Laura returned from the river. She told them that they would have time before supper to go sliding, and she had a fresh seal poke that they could use as a sled. A seal poke was made out of the skin of a hair seal, and Susie wanted the children to use it as a sled because the powdery snow would make the seal poke very clean. Susie used seal pokes for making footwear, and sometimes she stored seal oil or whale oil in them. They could also be used to store dried caribou and seal meat.

After dinner, Willy settled down to study. Since the family did not have electricity, he lit one of the kerosene lanterns and sat down in front of the stove to keep warm. Willy was a good student, and he enjoyed learning about places and ideas that took him beyond the village where he lived. Sometimes he was puzzled by the contrast between his home and what he learned at school, but he was eager to know more about the places described in the books he read.

Candle, Alaska.

After school was let out in the spring, Willy and his family moved from Candle to Bear Creek, a summer mining camp. This was an exciting time. The long Arctic nights had given way to long hours of daylight. The river was beginning to creak and groan as the ice started to break.

"Hey, Willy! Give me a hand with the dogs," Willy's father called.

Willy rushed over. His dad had a good team of dogs. They were fast and could travel long distances. The sled they would pull was piled high with the things the family would need for their stay in Bear Creek. But the dogs were excited, and it was hard to get them in their harness. The lead dog was especially troublesome, but Willy, who was now old enough to help his father, was able to quiet the animal enough to harness it. Finally, amidst much shouting and barking, the family set off.

Bear Creek was not far from Candle, but traveling was slow and it took several days on the trail to reach the town. Willy's family camped out on the trail, wrapping themselves in warm bedrolls at night and burrowing into the snow.

Since it was a summer mining town, most of the people staying in Bear Creek spent the season living in tents. During the summer the town bustled with activity, but when Willy and his family arrived, the work was just getting started. Miners were coming into Bear Creek from all over the world, hoping to get rich on gold. Many, like Jack Beltz, had been there before.

Willy liked to wander around listening to the tales some of the men told. There were places so different from those he knew, places with many more people than any town he had ever seen—places such as the ones he saw in the movies or read about in books. Someday, he wanted to really see them.

In the meantime, though, summer here was a lot of fun. The children fished for grayling and trout, and sold the fish in town. When they weren't fishing, Willy and his brothers and sisters could sail down the Kiwalik River on bread pans, sometimes for miles, depending on what they used for a sail. In the summer months, the sun was shining most of the time, so Willy and his brothers and sisters spent hours outside hunting and fishing and sailing to make up for the long winter months when they had to spend so much time inside.

At the end of the summer, Willy's father built a large raft with three decks for sailing down the river to Candle for the winter. One deck was for the dogs, one deck was for cooking, and the other deck was for sleeping. On the way down the river, Willy's father shot moose and caribou for the winter supply of food. The family spent several days floating down the river. When they finally arrived in Candle, they moved everything back into the cabin and used the raft for firewood for the winter.

As the days became shorter and colder, Willy knew winter was on its way. Soon it would be time for school to start. He was now sixteen and had graduated from the eighth grade. Much of what Willy had learned had been self-taught, and even though he had only finished the eighth grade, he already had more education than most Alaskan whites. Most of the Eskimos and Indians in northern Alaska had no education at all. Three-quarters of the villages and little towns in northern Alaska had no school. Willy knew that he had been lucky.

Even though he didn't know what he wanted to do when he grew older, Willy wanted to be able to choose wisely, and he wanted to be good at whatever he did choose. It was important that he stay in school.

Candle had no high school, and besides, the family was moving to Haycock, another mining town in the North. Haycock did not have a high school either. In fact, the closest high school was in Nome, Alaska, about eighty miles away from Haycock. Willy knew, from talking with other people, that in other parts of the world there were schools in every town, and in some towns there were even colleges and universities. He thought that there should be more schools in Alaska so that everyone could have a chance to be educated.

Meanwhile, there was still the problem of going to high school. Willy decided to talk with Mrs. Ausley, the grade school teacher in Haycock. She agreed to teach Willy for several hours each night.

The next problem was books. Willy had some money saved from the summer, but not nearly enough for books, which had to be ordered specially from Nome. When he set about finding work, he found that he could make money in his spare time by cutting wood. He also became the grade school janitor and worked evenings after school.

Two years later, Willy completed the tenth grade. Although he did not have all the education he wanted, he felt he could teach himself. And besides, he was restless and eager to see more of the world. A friend had told him about Hollywood, where they made those movies that had always fascinated Willy. He decided to go there and get a job building sets for the movie companies.

California is about three thousand miles away from northern Alaska. (It is about the same distance as from the East Coast to the West Coast of the United States.) Since there were no roads out of Alaska—not even a railroad going to the southern states—the fastest way to California was by boat.

It was a long trip. Finally, after several weeks at sea, the boat docked in Los Angeles, California. Los Angeles was by far the biggest city Willy had ever seen, and he was filled with admiration. He was very excited as he made his way to Hollywood and started to look for a job.

Willy had not realized that the Great Depression had hit the entire country, and there were no jobs and no money around. He spent weeks looking for a job—finally, any job—but no matter how hard he looked, he could find nothing.

At last Willy's money ran out. Like many others, he joined the bread lines simply to keep from starving to death. It did not take long for him to decide that the best thing to do would be to return to Alaska. He managed to borrow enough money for the fare and boarded a ship leaving California. Life was hard in Alaska too, and jobs were difficult to find, but Willy knew he could make a living there.

CHAPTER V

The Bear

In 1940, near the end of the Depression, Will had been back in Alaska nine years. They had been exciting years. Will had worked first as a chain man for a survey crew, then as a laborer, and finally he had decided to learn carpentry as a trade. By the time the Depression ended, Will had traveled throughout northern Alaska, working and making friends wherever he went. He was becoming an excellent carpenter, and he was a strong member of the Carpenters Union.

In 1934, Will had married Helen Merryfield, a school friend with whom he had grown up in Candle. They had three children: George, Carolyn, and Wanda.

Will worked hard as a carpenter, but when he got home at night, he spent as much time as he could with his children. He told George and Carolyn, who were old enough to understand, stories of the work he did and tales of the Arctic that he remembered from his childhood.

"All right, Carolyn, I'll tell you a story tonight," he said one evening. Will was tired, and there was still sawdust in his hair. Even though he was young—still in his twenties—ten hours of carpentry were enough to make him glad to be home.

A traditional Eskimo dance: the hunter describes the perils of the chase.

"Once upon a time," he began, "there was a whale hunter named Noatak. Noatak had a great harpoon. The shaft was carved from the jawbone of a whale, and the point was made of ivory tusk from the giant walrus."

The children listened, their eyes shining as if they saw right past their father, as if they saw the hunter Noatak and his great harpoon.

Will's mind raced ahead of the story. He spoke with feeling, but his mind was not in the Eskimo past, because he was looking at the future. His future, and his children's, would be far different from the old days. Never again could anyone live as the Eskimos had lived in the days of Noatak. "A great bear had attacked Noatak's village and had eaten several children and one of the old people. All of the men were at sea, hunting the whales that had come early that spring. Noatak was with them in the first boat. He was sure to catch a whale since he had the best harpoon and the strongest arm. The men were far away at sea when they saw a boat approaching them. It was a messenger boat that had been sent by the villagers to warn the hunters that the village had been attacked by a great bear. The oldest boys from the village were paddling the boat."

Little Carolyn's eyes were focused on the fire. She seemed to be hypnotized by the words of the story. Her big brother George had closed his eyes. He was wondering if he would have been chosen to paddle the messenger boat.

Will was thinking of how the Eskimos' lives were changing and how the Eskimo people could no longer control the way they lived. The Eskimos had come to need money in order to survive, even though they had lived in Alaska without money for thousands of years.

Will went on with his story. "The men had a council meeting right on the ocean. They lashed their boats together and made speeches. One after another, they spoke. One man said they should all return to save their children. Another said that not all the men were needed, so only a few should go. A third said they should stay at sea since the village was almost starving and needed whale meat.

"Finally Noatak spoke. He said that everyone had spoken honestly and well. He agreed that the village needed meat and that the children must be saved from the bear and that only a few should return, perhaps only one.

"The men in the boats became restless. No one wanted to face the great bear alone. Noatak stepped into the messenger boat with his great harpoon and vowed that he would not return until he had destroyed the bear.

"But the men called to him, saying that without him they were not certain they could catch enough whales for the winter. Noatak promised that he would return before the whales had gone. Then he paddled off so powerfully that the boat made large waves."

Little George and Carolyn were thinking that Noatak should hurry before the bear ate any more children, while Will thought to himself how money was the enemy now—money was the bear that had come to attack the Eskimo way of life. There must be a way to control the changes that money was making in the lives of the Eskimos.

"Noatak arrived at the village. All the people were hiding in their huts, and all the doors were locked. There were tracks of the great bear all over the village. He had eaten the village's supply of fish and torn apart several of the small boats. The people inside were afraid to come out even when they heard Noatak's voice. He went from house to house, hoping to get some information. Suddenly he heard the bear behind him. Dropping his harpoon, he turned and drew his knife. The bear was surprised. Instead of running, Noatak was facing him. Quickly Noatak sunk the knife into the great bear. The bear groaned and turned to run. Noatak picked up his harpoon and began the chase. He knew that the wounded bear was more dangerous than he had been before.

"It was a long, long chase, beyond the Eskimos' lands, across the Tanana Valley, all the way to the Yukon. The chase lasted many days and nights until finally the great bear became too tired to run. By then they were far north in the Yukon.

"Noatak, the whale hunter, lifted his great harpoon. He

was tired, too. His muscles strained to the breaking point as he threw. The bear reared up. He was ready to fight, ready to die, and determined to destroy Noatak.

"The great harpoon hit the bear like a falling tree. The brown giant fell backwards, dead."

The children were glad that the story ended happily for the Eskimo people. But Will knew that the days when problems could be solved by killing an enemy were over. Somehow he would have to learn a different way to protect his family and his people. Not even Noatak himself would have been any help with today's problems.

"But this is not the end of the story," Will said. "Noatak had promised to return for the whale hunt. Without his arm and harpoon, his village would have too little whale meat to last the long winter. But he was hundreds of miles from his village and it was already late.

"Noatak took his harpoon and hurled it into the earth. A spring of water popped out of the earth where the harpoon landed. It formed a stream and then a river. Noatak made a kayak from the skin of the great bear and paddled down this river to his village. And that was how the mighty Yukon River came to be and why it runs from the Yukon through Alaska into the Bering Sea.

"Noatak arrived back in time for the whaling season. With his help, the village was well supplied with whale meat for the entire winter."

Will rocked silently in his chair. Carolyn was asleep in his arms. He thought how lucky Noatak had been. The old ways were disappearing, and the new ways were too strange for the people to understand. Having little respect for those who had not learned how to handle money, white business

Will as a young man.

people often cheated the Eskimos. As the Eskimos were losing control of their lives, they were also losing their self-respect. Somehow money had brought this about. A man cannot kill money as he can kill a bear. Will knew that the people needed some kind of protection, and they needed to be better educated.

Sitting in his chair, he looked at his hands, hardened by work, and then he looked up at the calendar. It was 1940, he was twenty-eight years old, and much had happened in Alaska since the Depression. One important change was the growth of unions. He himself had joined the Carpenters Union. Because it made legal agreements with construction companies, the union had a say in what the carpenters' wages and working conditions would be. There were other advantages for the union member. A health plan guaranteed the member money to pay medical expenses for himself and his family.

Will believed that the union was a way to have some

control over the changes that money was making in the Eskimo life. He wondered how he could help direct the Carpenters Union. Then he began to think about whether it would be possible for him to have some control over the forces that were changing the lives of all the people of northern Alaska, both Eskimo and white.

Will fell asleep and dreamed of Noatak. The whale hunter had become a leader of all the unions. He was wearing a parka made of bear skin, and he held his harpoon in his left hand. And in his right hand was the legal agreement that assured all the workers a decent wage and a safe place to work.

CHAPTER VI

Alaska in Wartime

It was December 1941. The one main street of Nome was dark, and the snow glittered in the freezing weather. A cold wind was blowing in off the Bering Sea.

Will Beltz stepped out into the cold morning. He made his way down the boardwalk which ran along the row of huddled houses. Off to one side, a team of sled dogs lay curled up in the snow.

Will was on his way downtown to get news of jobs here or in Fairbanks. He and his family had moved to Nome from Fairbanks, but Will still traveled back and forth between the two towns to do carpentry work. By now he was an excellent carpenter, but in the wintertime work was scarce, and the men were kept inside by the temperature.

This morning it was thirty degrees below zero. Will hurried into a cafe, and the warmth there felt good. The men inside were excited and talking loudly. A man called Will over.

"Will! The Japanese attacked Pearl Harbor. We're in the war."

"It's going to be a long war," one of the men said. "But Alaska is a long way from Germany or Japan."

Will thought differently. He had educated himself well

Fishing through the winter ice near King Island Village at Nome, Alaska.

and he had been to the states. He knew that things there were very different from here in Alaska. The war, he reflected, would have a great effect on Alaska. Alaska was the only part of the United States that was not protected from attack. The federal government in Washington, D.C., had never considered Alaska important enough to give it very much attention.

In fact, while the rest of the United States had Army, Navy, and Air Force bases for protection, Alaska had only one small Army base. While the rest of the United States had roads and airports so that people could travel, Alaska had very few roads or airports and people had a hard time getting about. Though it was twice the size of Texas, Alaska had fewer miles of highway than the smallest state in the union, Rhode Island.

Will simply could not understand this. Now the country was at war with Germany and Japan, and Alaska was closer to Japan than any part of the United States, even the Hawaiian Islands. The easiest way for the Japanese to invade the United States was through Alaska, and yet Alaska was not protected. Will knew that now things would have to change.

"Maybe you think Alaska is a long way from the war, but that is just not true," Will said.

The men listened, for they knew Will had traveled and seen more than most people in Alaska, and he was known to be an honest and intelligent man.

Will went on. "The war is going to change Alaska. The rest of the country is going to have to start paying attention to us. Alaska is important."

Even Will did not know just how important Alaska

would be. By the end of the war, billions of dollars had poured into Alaska. The number of soldiers stationed in Alaska increased from three thousand in 1940 to three million in 1945—a number greater than the population of the entire state. Roads and airports were built. During the war the Army built the Alcan Highway, which stretches from Fairbanks into British Columbia, connecting there with highways leading into the United States. Although it was only a gravel road, for the first time Alaska was connected overland with the mainland of the United States.

By 1942, what Will feared had come true. The Japanese had invaded the Aleutian Islands, that long string of islands that runs west off Alaska's coast. In 1942, two of the islands, Attu and Kiska, were captured by the Japanese. These two islands were the only part of our country to be invaded by anyone during World War II. When they were taken, the United States government came to realize the importance of such seemingly unimportant areas as Alaska. Men and supplies came flooding into the territory, and in 1943 the Japanese were driven away.

In 1942, Will traveled to Gambell, a small Army outpost on St. Lawrence Island, to build housing for the federal government. St. Lawrence Island lies about 175 miles west of Nome in the Bering Sea. It was March and still wintertime on the island. Spring would not come for another two months. Will was hard at work putting up buildings despite the cold.

A Japanese submarine had been patrolling the island continually, and it showed no indication of leaving. The ship that was to bring Gambell desperately needed supplies had been unable to get through because of the submarine.

Umiaks such as this one are still used in Gambell for hunting.

Will knew that if something were not done, the people would very likely starve to death. Even though Alaska has a coastline longer than the Atlantic, the Pacific, and the Gulf coasts of the forty-eight states combined, it was almost totally unprotected. Gambell was in serious trouble.

It was at this time that Will met Maj. Muktuk Marston. Major Marston had spent the war years organizing the Alaska Territorial Guard, and it was for this reason that he was in Gambell in March 1942. Marston had enormous respect for the Eskimos, for they were experts at surviving in the Arctic and were willing and eager to help in the war effort. They made ideal soldiers for that part of the world. Few other men, however, appreciated their value, since most outsiders knew nothing about the problems of survival in the harsh climate of northern Alaska.

Both Will Beltz and Major Marston realized the danger that Gambell faced. The village had to get food, so Will and Major Marston decided to get the men together for a seal-hunting expedition. This would not be easy because the people were already weak from hunger. Soon no one would have enough strength to do anything. Will and the major quickly called the men of the village together and selected the crew for the hunt.

When the men began to get their dog teams together, they found that the dogs were too weak to pull the sleds. Will and Major Marston decided that they would have to kill one hundred of the dogs and use them for food for the other dogs. The animals were killed, and soon the remaining dogs were strong enough for the hunt. Warm clothes were made from the butchered dogs' skins, and the men set out to hunt the seals for the villagers.

The hunt was a big success. The men returned with enough seal meat to keep the villagers alive for some time. Eventually the Japanese submarine left the area, and the supply ship did arrive. Major Marston departed soon after for other villages to continue organizing the Alaska Territorial Guard.

Will returned to Nome later that year after finishing the building project in Gambell. He continued to work through the last years of the war putting up much-needed housing in northern Alaska. Wherever he went, he saw the huge changes the war was bringing to the territory. These changes, Will thought, would affect Eskimos and Indians and whites alike, as more and more people wanted the kinds of things that could be gotten so easily in the states. Better roads, more schools and hospitals, and better housing were needed.

Will knew that the unions were a big help in getting better jobs for the workers. But who could begin to help people who needed a school or a hospital? Could one person help an entire village, or several villages, get needed doctors, medicine, and good food? Both the government of Alaska and the government in Washington, D.C., should be concerned about the people of the territory. As he worried about the different problems of the people in Alaska, Will began to think about what political action he himself could take.

CHAPTER VII

Will Runs for Office

In 1948, Will ran for the territorial house of representatives. For years, friends in northern Alaska had urged him to get into politics. He was respected in all of the villages he had visited because of his honesty and his deep concern for the territory. A year before the 1948 election, Will decided to follow their advice. One major reason for his decision was the success of his friend, Frank Peratrovich, in getting an antidiscrimination bill passed in the territorial legislature. Frank's achievement is a story in itself.

Frank Peratrovich was part Tlingit Indian, and he lived in Klawock in southeastern Alaska. Frank took a government job in Juneau, the capital of the territory, in 1940. Everywhere he traveled in Anchorage and Juneau, he saw signs in shops and restaurants saying: "Whites only. We do not cater to Indian trade."

Something was very wrong. The Indians and Eskimos of Alaska were fighting for their country in World War II. They were the original inhabitants of Alaska. The land had belonged to them for centuries. Yet people now were saying that Indians and Eskimos were not as good as whites. This was simply and obviously not true.

Will, too, had faced some of the same kinds of discrimination that Frank Peratrovich met in southeastern Alaska. Eskimos in Nome were not allowed to enter some restaurants; they had to sit in a special place in the movie theater; and they had a hard time getting good jobs. This was not fair, but Will did not become angry or bitter. Instead, he tried to show the men he met that people should be judged individually, not by race.

A group of men, Frank Peratrovich among them, began to push to get a bill passed in the legislature that would make discrimination against Indians and Eskimos illegal. It was a hard fight. Many of the legislators did not believe that such a law was necessary.

Opinions began to change gradually. Stories came to the territorial government in Juneau describing Eskimos and Indians who could not get jobs. According to one report, an Eskimo girl in Nome had been bodily thrown out of a restaurant when she tried to get served. The governor of the territory, Ernest Gruening, helped in the fight against discrimination. In 1943, a bill to end discrimination was hotly debated in the territorial legislature. When it finally came to a vote, the bill was defeated by a tie. More work was necessary to get such a measure passed.

Frank Peratrovich decided to run for the house of representatives. In 1945, he was elected from his district in southeastern Alaska. He was now in a position to add his vote to the cause. In that year, the first antidiscrimination bill was passed in the territory of Alaska.

Will was encouraged by Frank's success. Politics offered a way to change some of the more pressing problems in the North. Through politics, Will might have a chance to fight for more schools and houses, and better jobs for everyone —Eskimos, Indians, and whites—in northern Alaska. He knew it would not be easy.

Before entering politics, Will had met with some disappointing failures. Once he had tried to get a loan for a housing project in Nome. Housing is a major problem in the Arctic. The winters are cruel, and it is very important that families have strong, warm houses to live in. Unfortunately, many did not. Despite the fact that housing was so desperately needed, Will's application was turned down because he was half Eskimo. Will reflected that a man in politics would have the influence necessary to see that things which needed doing in his district got done.

On election night, Will and a group of friends gathered together to listen to the election returns. These were coming in slowly because many of the villages did not have phones or wireless radios, and they had to mail in the election results the next day. A day later, everyone knew that Will had won. He was now a member of the Alaska territorial house of representatives. His career in government had begun.

CHAPTER VIII

Taxes and Fair Wages

Will Beltz went to Juneau in 1949 to take his place in the territorial house of representatives. Juneau lies in southeastern Alaska, over a thousand miles from Nome. The city is perched on a small piece of land between mountains and water, and tall, craggy mountains tower above it. In 1949, many of the people in Juneau who were not working for the government earned a living fishing, and fishing boats were docked at the piers year round. The smell of cool sea air and the bustle of a government town greeted Will as he got off the plane. Southeastern Alaska was truly a different place from the interior where Will lived and worked.

Will was eager to begin his career in politics. In fact, he was to be a part of the most vigorous and productive legislature in the history of Alaska. A new direction and a new surge toward statehood and economic stability were to mark the next ten years of Alaskan history. Will was to be a major actor in the drama.

The 1946 legislature had been a disaster. The territory had spent four million dollars more than it had been able to raise. Worse yet, there seemed to be no way to obtain the much-needed money for the territorial government,

47 TAXES AND FAIR WAGES

since Alaska was "owned" by outsiders who took the money home to the states, leaving little in the territory. Every summer, miners, fishermen, and construction workers came to Alaska to work. At the end of the season they left with the thousands of dollars they had earned in Alaska. Since the wealth was taken away each year by non-Alaskans, the territory was not able to benefit from its own natural resources. Angered by this situation, the voters had made a clean sweep in the 1948 election and elected new representatives for the Alaskan government.

Will knew that the problems of schools and housing and bad health, which he saw in every town and village he visited, were the problems of the territory as a whole. But it took more than talk to get things done. Will's experience told him one of the first things they needed was money. It took a lot of money to build a school, or send a doctor to a village, or build a hospital.

The 1949 legislature passed bills that made it possible for the government to stop money from leaving Alaska. Some of the money taken out each year by non-Alaskans was to be taxed so the territory would have the funds to spend on its own problems. By the time this session was adjourned, Will could say that the government was on its way out of debt.

Other important issues were being raised. The most pressing issue of the next ten years, the years Will spent in government, was statehood. Should Alaska govern itself? Should Alaska progress with the rest of the United States?

In 1945, Ernest Gruening, governor of the territory, had asked the legislature to put a question to the voters the following election year: "Should Alaska become a state?"

Although the majority was not overwhelming, the votes showed that Alaskans did want their territory to become a state.

Now Governor Gruening felt he could go ahead with the plans to push for statehood. During the legislative session in 1949, a committee was set up to work for statehood. Will's friend, Frank Peratrovich, was appointed to the committee. Will himself became deeply involved with the drive for statehood, as did many of the legislators elected to the 1949 session.

Throughout its history, the major decisions affecting Alaska had been made by people who had little knowledge of the territory. For instance, the fisheries, which were a major Alaskan resource, were being supervised by the federal government. Slowly, the fishing was being ruined, for it was not always possible for someone in Washington, D.C., to know what should be done several thousand miles away in Alaska. Even more damaging to the welfare of the region was the fact that while Alaska was being governed by the federal government, it did not even have one voting representative in that government. A delegate from Alaska was allowed to sit in the national legislature, but he could not vote. Many people believed that Alaska should be allowed to govern itself and have a voice in the decisions made by Congress.

Wherever Will went in his district, he explained the importance of seeking statehood. By the end of the 1949 legislature, great strides had been made, and the statehood movement was officially underway. This movement and Alaska's improved economic situation were encouraging to Will, and after completing his two-year term in the house of representatives in 1950, he ran for the territorial senate.

Although he had little money for campaigning, Will wrote letters to the people in his district, asking them to send him back to Juneau. He won the election in 1950 and bcame a senator in the territorial government. In 1954 and 1958 he was reelected. Will never lost an election from his district in northern Alaska.

The Indians and Eskimos were truly caught between two cultures in the 1950s, as they are even today. The money and goods of white society had no place in their traditional way of life. People supported themselves from the land. They killed their own food and built their own houses from

Old ways and new in Nome.

what was at hand. They lived in small villages, and an individual's success was determined by how much he or she could give to the village. But now, another way of life intruded upon the traditional culture. White business men and women sold goods from their world to the native Alaskans. It became increasingly necessary to have money. How well one worked with others was not so important anymore. It seemed that in the white world, the mark of a person's success was how much money he or she alone could make.

One of the ways of helping people to change was through schools. Will remembered how hard it had been for him to get an education. When he was ready for high school, there was no school for him to attend. Everyone, white, Eskimo, or Indian, should have an equal chance to get a good education. All the years he was in government, Will worked to provide money for education and to make scholarships available for people in the state, especially Eskimos and Indians, who wanted to finish high school and perhaps go to a college or university.

As he saw the ever-increasing need for money, Will also became concerned about jobs and labor conditions in the North. Good jobs that paid enough to support a family were scarce. Many of the Indians and Eskimos in Alaska lived on less than fifteen hundred dollars a year, an amount less than many people in the United States paid for a car. Because so many things had to be shipped hundreds of miles into the interior of Alaska, or even thousands of miles from the states, everything cost more. The combination of high prices and low wages caused widespread poverty among native Alaskans.

Will and his sister Laura in Fairbanks.

A partial answer to this, Will still believed, was in the unions, which could help people to find jobs that paid fair wages. Eskimos and Indians often had a difficult time getting into unions. Will decided that the way to change this was for him to become involved in the union leadership.

Soon Will became the head of the Carpenters Union in Fairbanks, Alaska's third largest city. Since his area of control also covered Nome and other towns and villages in northwest Alaska, he was able to travel around to give encouragement and advice. He urged people to get into trade unions, and he helped to make it easier for them to join. He bargained for higher wages and tried to make sure that the working conditions were good, that people were not overworked, and that safety rules were followed.

In 1955, Will was elected president of the Alaska Council of Carpenters, and thus he became the leader for carpenters in the territory as a whole. Today, he is remembered as one of the great leaders of the union.

CHAPTER IX

President of the First State Senate

The 1950s were busy years for Will. His time was divided between the union and politics, and many things were happening. The drive for statehood, started officially in the 1949 legislature, was gaining speed. Will heartily lent his energy to the cause.

Because Alaska was not a state, the governor of the territory was not elected by the people of Alaska. Instead, he was appointed by the president of the United States. Will and many others in Alaska were afraid that another man would be appointed to replace Governor Gruening, who was a driving force behind the movement for statehood. No one wanted to see the governor leave Alaska. But Ernest Gruening was a Democrat, and a Republican president (President Eisenhower) had been elected in 1952. There was a good chance the president would want to appoint a Republican governor of Alaska.

In 1953, a delegation was selected to go to Washington, D.C., to urge that Gruening remain governor of Alaska. Will was part of the delegation and made the long trip to the East Coast of the United States. The men told President Eisenhower that Gruening was a dedicated man who had governed Alaska for almost twenty years. He knew the problems of Alaska, and he understood what the territory needed. But in the end President Eisenhower appointed another man.

Will was disappointed. He had supported Governor Gruening from the time he first entered the territorial legislature, and he feared that the loss of Ernest Gruening would be a real loss to Alaska. However, Gruening remained in Alaska to work for statehood. He also spent much time during the next few years persuading people around the country that Alaska should be made a state.

When Will returned from Washington, D.C., to Fairbanks, he met Arne Louise Bulkely, a woman who would later become his wife. Will's first marriage had ended in divorce several years before. Like Will, Arne was interested in the welfare of the Alaskan people. She had come to Alaska from New York to work with the Public Health Service as a nurse. She had been in Alaska four years, working in the southeastern part before moving to Fairbanks where she met Will. Because many places in Alaska had no doctor or nurse, Arne often had complete responsibility for the care of the people in the towns and villages she visited.

Arne and Will were married on November 28, 1953. In 1955, their first son, Mark, was born. Later Arne and Will were to have two more sons, Billy and Axel, and a daughter, Kathy.

Will worked for the Carpenters Union until 1955. Two years later, he and his family moved to Unalakleet. The village lies on the west coast of Alaska. It is bordered by the Bering Sea and is just 150 miles from Nome across Norton Sound. Will's friend Major Marston had described

Unalakleet as the "garden spot of Alaska." It is beautiful. Pointed blue mountains rise in the distance, and green, rolling hills surround the village. Unlike much of northern Alaska, the soil around Unalakleet is not frozen beneath the surface, and so it can be farmed. About five hundred people, most of them Eskimos and Indians, lived there in the 1950s. One central street ran between the low cabins and the few larger frame houses.

Will and his family settled into the large white frame house that also served as the town's health clinic. With running water and electricity, it was one of the most modern houses in town. Arne opened the health clinic, and Will went to work as a maintenance man. What Will really wanted to do in Unalakleet was to establish a homestead. In 1957, Major Marston obtained 160 acres of land for Will. The land was about ten miles from town, and rivers ran down both sides of the land to Unalakleet. Will hoped to grow potatoes and float them downstream to supply all the villagers. Will was a better politician than he was a farmer, however, and he was never able to clear enough land to fulfill the homesteading requirements so that he would own the land free and clear.

In the meantime, Will became more and more involved in his work in politics. In 1955 a constitution was drawn up to be used when Alaska became a state. The growing weight of opinion was that Alaska must take its place in the union. The territory was becoming more and more economically stable. With the efforts of legislators like Will, it had been able to start working to improve the welfare of its citizens.

Elsewhere, there was still much opposition to statehood.

Many people in the United States did not think Alaska was ready to become a state. Some felt that Alaska was much better governed as a territory, with control in the hands of the federal government.

Will disagreed completely. The people of Alaska best understood their own problems, and they could best handle them, too. At one point, Will was asked to testify before a committee holding a hearing on the statehood issue. When one of the senators from the states asked if Will thought that decisions in Alaska were being made by people who did not fully understand local problems, he answered, "Precisely, yes."

By 1958, Will had served one term in the territorial house of representatives, and two terms in the territorial senate. During those nine years, Alaskans had launched a concentrated drive to gain statehood, and finally, in 1958, the time had come. A statehood bill was presented in Congress. The bill would have to pass both houses of Congress if Alaska were to become a state. The bill first went to the House of Representatives, where it finally was passed on May 28, 1958, after several days of heated debate. The bill went to the Senate where strong attempts were also made to defeat or sidetrack the bill. When it came to a vote at last, on June 30, 1958, it was obvious that the bill's supporters were in the majority. All the years of effort had paid off. The newspaper Will picked up the next morning proclaimed in banner headlines, "Alaska—49th State in the Union."

Will was reelected again in 1958 for another four-year term in the Senate. Everyone hoped the state's first legislative session would herald great accomplishments.

On the opening day of the Senate's first session, the chairman rapped his gavel on the speaker's stand. "Will the Senate of the *State* of Alaska please come to order." The chamber quieted down, and the chairman proceeded with the business of the first day.

One of the first items on the agenda was the election of the Senate president. This man would handle and direct all sessions of the Senate, and he would see that the business of the Senate proceeded in an orderly fashion. In fact, much of the success of the Senate's work would rest on his shoulders. Will had hoped to be elected Senate president in 1957, but another legislator had won instead. He was unsure about his chances today.

Nominations from the floor of the Senate were called for. Frank Peratrovich, Will's friend, was nominated first. Then Frank himself rose to nominate Will Beltz. No other nominations were made. Before Will had much time to wonder how the election would turn out, the vote was called for.

Both Frank and Will were outstanding representatives of the Eskimo and Indian populations. Both were respected by everyone who knew them, and both had served the Senate for many years. In spite of their equally strong records, Will was elected unanimously. Frank Peratrovich, as well as every other member of the Senate, had voted for him. Will had been elected president of Alaska's first state Senate.

Will's election was a great tribute from his fellow senators. No other gesture could show so well the respect they had for Will. Republicans and Democrats alike had voted for him, and they had voted well, for in the following months, Will proved to be an outstanding president. Arne once asked what he was thinking so hard about each night. "I'm thinking about everything that could possibly happen in the Senate tomorrow and what I would do," replied Will.

Unfortunately, Will was destined to die at the peak of his career, at the early age of forty-eight. It was 1960; and Will had returned to Juneau after spending the summer and fall at his homestead in Unalakleet. Once again that January, Will took his seat as Senate President.

One day in March, as Will presided over debate in the Senate chamber, he suddenly slumped forward on his desk. Will's colleagues rushed to the president's platform, and moments later Will regained consciousness. He was led from the chamber, and a doctor was called. Later, Will returned and finished his term as president that session.

But the first signs of a brain tumor had emerged that March day. Doctors operated twice that spring and summer, but to no avail. Will entered the Alaska Native Hospital in Anchorage in September and died two months later.

Will devoted his life to the people of Alaska. He proved

Will's cabin near Unalakleet where he homesteaded just before his death.

himself an able representative and an outstanding union leader. He was equally at home at a formal government reception or exchanging tales with villagers living near the Bering Sea. He liked to listen and was able to consider seriously the problems and concerns of others. After his death, his efforts in education were memorialized when the regional high school in Nome, the first of its kind in northern Alaska, was named the William E. Beltz High School. Today, more than ten years after his death, Will Beltz is remembered as one of Alaska's outstanding leaders, a spokesman who stood above race and personal interest.

Since Will's death, a new wave of native leaders has left its mark on the state's history. After a ten-year struggle, native Alaskans won just compensation for the land the white people had settled. In 1971 Congress passed the Alaska Native Claims Settlement Act, a law that made it possible, at long last, for native Alaskans to become leaders in state business and politics. The act gave Alaskan natives title to 40 million acres of land and provided for a cash settlement of $1 billion.

The money and land were given to native groups to administer through twelve regional corporations and a flock of village corporations. Although poverty is still widespread, native corporations have launched successful businesses throughout the state, and many native leaders have served in the state legislature.

THE AUTHOR

Ellen Wolfe is a newswriter and reporter for the Associated Press in Anchorage, Alaska. One of three AP staff members in Alaska, she is responsible for reporting news of both statewide and national interest.

Ms. Wolfe earned a B.A. degree at Washington State University and an M.S. at the University of Oregon. She has been an Associated Press reporter in Seattle, Washington, and Juneau, Alaska, and has worked for the *Southeast Alaska Empire,* a daily newspaper in Juneau. She has also worked in Fairbanks, Alaska, for the *Tundra Times,* a bi-monthly newspaper which publishes news about and of interest to Alaskan natives.

The photographs are reproduced through the courtesy of the Alaska Department of Economic Development; the University of Alaska, Fairbanks; and Laura Wright.

OTHER BIOGRAPHIES
IN THIS SERIES ARE

Robert Bennett
Joseph Brant
Crazy Horse
Geronimo
LaDonna Harris
Oscar Howe
Ishi
Chief Joseph
Maria Martinez
Billy Mills
George Morrison
Michael Naranjo
Osceola
Powhatan
Red Cloud
Sacajawea
Sequoyah
Sitting Bull
Maria Tallchief
Tecumseh
Jim Thorpe
Pablita Velarde
William Warren
Annie Wauneka